PLAYING TECHNIQUES & PERFORMANCE STUDIES

For Trumpet

Basic Techniques and Concepts for Developing a Solid Foundation

TABLE OF CONTENTS

Cover Photo by Carol Weinberg

HAL•LEONARD CORPORATION

7777 W. BLUEMOUND RD. P.O. BOX 13819 MILWAUKEE, WI 53213

Introduction

I feel extremely happy and pleased that Hal Leonard has called on me to do this work. This is a book that I have always dreamed of writing and to which I have dedicated a great part of my life. All the information that I have learned and collected throughout so many years of study and performing with great masters has yielded this valuable gift.

I do not pretend either to create anything new or to introduce in a new way what has already been discovered. What I want is to share with you my experiences and my personal daily routines. You should take advantage of them, and, at the same time, you can interpret them. That is my goal!

I have to admit that the trumpet is a difficult instrument to learn, but not an impossible one. Everything depends on your dedication, perseverance, and passion to learn and improve until you acquire a solid technique. Technique is the vehicle that permits you to interpret your feelings. Moreover, technique is what allows you to share your God-given talent with the audience.

The main goals are always these: to be "ready," to interpret the music well, to touch the heart of the audience, and to send a clean, neat, and definite message. This is the purpose of daily practice.

I have been asked about the amount of time required to study, and I repeatedly say that *there is no time limit*. What is most important is to balance the time you have to study in such a way that you can cover all the necessary topics. You have to practice *flexibility, long tones, crescendos and decrescendos, articulations* (particularly staccato), *intervals, arpeggios,* and *scales* (in all keys and with various articulations). These are the things that will be needed at concert time.

As I already mentioned, the main goal is to be *prepared*, because you never know what you are going to find on the music stand. In the recording studio, for example, no one ever knows ahead of time what musical tasks await them. Therefore, readiness is crucial.

Remember, too, that the time for practice can never be measured in terms of hours or minutes, of effort or sacrifice. What is important is the *quality* (concentration and *how* you practice), not the quantity of time measured on a clock.

There are some players that practice many hours. By the time they finish, their lips are completely exhausted and are left in a deplorable state. This impedes them from facing a performance, because their practice routine has destroyed the muscles, rather than strengthened them.

The purpose of practicing is to "build" and to actually feel *better* at the end of the session. In my opinion, after practicing, you should be ready for a concert. If this is not so, your practice has not been productive, because it has not helped to train the tongue, the fingers, and all the muscles involved in playing and interpreting music. You should never arrive at the point of total exhaustion.

If you feel tired at the end of a practice session, the benefits you might expect will fail to materialize. You should feel in excellent condition and ready to concertize at the conclusion of practice.

Furthermore, an extremely rigid practice format, where you practice the same studies each day for a regulated period of time, does not work well. If you are feeling well, keep practicing and take on more difficult challenges. However, once you feel fatigued, *stop and rest*. Remember, the body does not respond the same every day; your physical disposition changes. Therefore, you will need to adjust the physical demands you make on yourself accordingly to obtain the best results.

If you do things intelligently and correctly (resting a few minutes each time you sense muscle fatigue), you will be able to practice more hours each day and will see improvement in every aspect of your playing.

Your musical expression will depend on the effort, seriousness, and responsibility you dedicate to your studies. These combined factors will enable you to acquire the technique and confidence needed for a musical performance.

The trumpet demands a very disciplined and constant training, which should be concentrated on each of the fundamental elements in order to develop a good technique.

Confidence is based exclusively on preparation. When you *do* prepare appropriately, you feel confident about the fact that your lips *will* respond to your demands, that your muscles will be in good shape, that your fingers *will* operate in unison. Because you have prepared, you are calm. If, on the other hand, you have omitted any aspect of technique, it will be reflected in a lack of confidence, nervousness, and accordingly a diminished performance.

Throughout the years, the only thing I have found to eliminate fear or stage fright is to feel certain that I have prepared correctly, that I know the music I am going to perform, that I have no doubts about fingerings or the keys I'm going to play in, and that my training has been done in a correct, serious, and responsible manner.

One of the most difficult things to accomplish once you become a professional will be to maintain the same love and enthusiasm to make music that you had at the beginning of your career. If that "true love" lasts, then you will surely feel the motivation to continue with your studies, rehearsals, and preparation until you decide to retire.

Since I feel that music has no limits, my opinion differs from those who think that once you have studied and learned, the need to review that which you have already learned is no longer important. The "high achievers" are those who keep the spirit of "eternal student." They never stop rehearsing or studying, in order to keep themselves in good musical shape. In my opinion, this is the attitude we, as musicians, should keep for our entire musical lives.

The trumpet is an instrument that possesses such incredible expressive power that, having chosen it, you should experience a mixture of joy, happiness, satisfaction, and pride.

Don't be afraid of its demands. On the contrary, enjoy the trumpet and find as much time as you can for it. Then you will really be able to enjoy the results.

When playing the trumpet, you'll observe that its penetrating sound travels; it grabs the audience's attention. Its sound transcends the entire orchestra. The excitement experienced by playing with control over a big, clean, and clear trumpet sound in an orchestra, or anywhere for that matter, is indescribable.

The voice a trumpet has within any musical group is very important. That's why you have to be sure about the quality of your performance. You have to be sure of what you do when on the stage because not only are good performances acclaimed, but also, the smallest errors can be heard. You can't go on stage without being prepared, warmed up properly, or feeling ready to make music.

In preparing this book I have included recorded examples from each section. I recorded them with a lot of enthusiasm and with the hope you will hear my points of view regarding sound, articulation, and interpretation. It should be understood that I do not consider my performance either the perfect way or the only way. It is only my point of view, my way of making music. It is a proposal and also a guide for those who are beginners and for professionals who might wish to share my musical way of thinking.

I have to say that one of the most beautiful things that music possesses is that it enables the instrumentalist to express his individual personality through the instrument. I can assure you that in no way do I desire to influence or obligate someone into thinking that my style of playing is either the only way or correct way. There are many interpretations, and all of them are legitimate when the intention is good and legitimate musical taste is exercised.

There is a long history of great trumpeters whose performances encompass the entire spectrum of conceptions and styles. I would not like to mention any one name, for it would surely result in leaving someone out. I just want to call them to your attention so you can ponder the greatness of music. Music allows room for everyone and for all the different styles.

My special recommendation regarding interpretation and style is to listen to all kinds of *good* music. There is only one kind of music: *good* music! Do not permit yourself to be influenced by those who tend to separate styles of music and musicians into small groups. The so-called "classical," "salsa," or "jazz" musicians are terms that I do not think are appropriate. To say "musicians" is enough. A *musician* is someone who makes music, loves music, and respects *all* the great writers of music and *all* musical styles.

Perhaps there could be a problem regarding the amount of musical education you have? The more learned you are through recordings, or about styles and musicians (artists on all instruments), the more your musical discretion will be enriched and likewise your musical readiness extended.

Always maintain the attitude of the "eternal student." Respect and admire all professionals and all the great artists on the trumpet, but don't think twice about approaching them to ask questions. Admiration and respect are necessary ingredients to becoming an artist. When you are able to admire and honor others, you will receive the same honor in return.

In this series, divided into three books, I have tried to include all the most important aspects necessary for the preparation of superlative technical and musical ability. Topics such as: *warm-up, pedal tones, staccato, intervals,* and *chromatic scales,* as well as a number of original pieces that will be useful for musical interpretation, are presented in an ordered progression.

I hope you'll enjoy this work, and that you will study it with the same amount of love that I have devoted to it throughout many years.

Keep in mind that your improvement will be measured by the amount of love you have for music, the instrument itself, and the profession.

Concerning Arban

Since Jean-Baptiste Arban published his trumpet method in 1864, it has been the foundation for practically all the great trumpet masters of the past and present, and surely will continue to be into the future. With this in mind, it is with great respect and love that I have included his studies in my method.

Note that the Arban book has not only been present in our libraries, but his legacy also resides in every refined trumpet performance. It is my opinion that no school of music should ignore such a valuable work.

General Advice

- Remember, if you are in a good frame of mind when you practice and the atmosphere is filled with enthusiasm, the benefits will be more positive and you will enjoy it more.

  It is necessary to learn how to enjoy practice. Try not to view practice as an obligation, but rather as a daily need for your spirit and training, a necessary part of your life.

- Practice at all the dynamic levels that are required to be played.

  I do not agree with the idea that one can practice at a single dynamic and then be able to play instantaneously at all volumes on a job. If you want to play at all dynamic levels, you must practice at all dynamic levels. It makes sense!

- Avoid the use of mutes in practice. Mutes distort the sound and the normal response of the trumpet.

- Avoid practicing in very "live" rooms with lots of reverberation. In echoing rooms, the sound appears to get bigger and rounder—in other words, more beautiful. Then when you face "reality" you realize, to your chagrin, how you've been deceived. Outside is a better place to practice!

  (For many years I practiced in a football stadium. I used to sit in the stands and project the sound toward the scoreboard. It worked well for me. Even though I did not play strongly, the sound flowed and I felt it stretch up to the other side of the field.)

- It is essential to practice not only at all volumes—piano, pianissimo, mezzo forte, fortissimo—but also to exercise the full range of the instrument by playing legato, staccato, triple- and double-tongued, with all the articulations at all the different intensities.

- Hold the instrument firmly with your left hand, preferably with the four fingers just inside the trumpet, around the valves and through the third valve ring, and the thumb passing through the first valve "saddle." The right hand should be soft, flexible, and yet dynamic, forceful, and ready to obey the commands coming from the brain directly to the fingers with exact precision.

- Take good care of your musical instrument. Keep it clean inside and out. Especially keep the mouthpiece clean, for reasons of health.

  The mouthpiece, valves, and slides should always be kept in "A-1" condition.

  Avoid denting the bell or leadpipe; it could radically change the sound and pitch of the instrument.

  Gig bags or soft cases are very convenient for travel, but do not really protect the instrument. I personally recommend the use of hard cases.

- Music practice should be music *reading* practice. You need to develop the habit of playing what you see on the printed page. This also makes the discipline of practice stricter and more organized and helps you to keep a record of your progress by showing how much you have covered and what is yet to be done. Later, of course, improvisation and memorization will be necessary skills to include in your practice day, but *reading* well is of primary importance.

  Reading music should become second nature. In fact, consciously thinking about the mechanics of reading music will be detrimental to your performance; it will make you sound much like a child does when first learning how to read a book.

- Use a metronome. Use it as often as you can. This is crucial. In addition, learn to move your hands as drummers do, and learn how to hold the sticks and use a practice pad. This is important not only for a general understanding of rhythm and coordination, but also to adapt to the "feel" of drummers and percussionists.

- Listen to and play all types of music. Don't discount anything; you need to learn all you can about music.

- Put into action the "golden rule" and do not criticize other musicians while they are playing. Nobody enjoys ridicule or criticism upon committing a mistake. What counts is that the musical piece being interpreted is evaluated according to its true intent and that the audience enjoys and appreciates it.

- A bit of advice for those playing in an ensemble: Be courteous to the other members of the orchestra. Don't turn your back during your colleagues' solos, and keep a pleasant attitude toward the audience throughout their performances.

- Your career demands the physical preparation of a high-performance athlete; therefore daily exercise is more than a need—it is a responsibility.

  Among the main physical concerns of a brass musician are the maintenance of the respiratory system, keeping the diaphragm muscle in excellent condition and under control, and staying in good shape overall.

  Drinking and smoking are bad for anybody, but for a wind musician they represent a disaster. Trumpet players in particular should avoid alcohol before a performance. Avoid any type of drugs! Drugs have destroyed many lives and potentially brilliant careers.

- A word about improvisation. Bach, Handel, Mozart—all improvised daily. Today, based on some badly mistaken suppositions, improvisation is reserved exclusively for "jazz" musicians. This is far from true. To improvise is to create music; it is to bring forward all the musical ideas that have been collected throughout the years and to share them with the audience at that very instant. I am also of a mind that improvisation of a cadenza, even in a concert, is valid. Remember, improvisation is not only a "jazz" matter, it is a *musician's* matter. A further example would be the aleatoric parts of avant garde music, or modern music, where improvisation on the musician's part is required. This is normal repertoire in "symphonic" orchestras!

- Learn to play in a section and have respect for the lead player by following him or her. Don't try to overshadow the lead voice. Your voice has its own important role in the harmony and needs to be played with enthusiasm and care.

  Remember that in an orchestra with three or four trumpets, all the voices are important within the chord. Any missing voice will make the chord sound different.

- Learn to use all type of mutes. Always have all of them with you when you go to a recording session or whenever you're called to play.

- By the same token, learn to play the flugelhorn and the piccolo trumpet; the ability to "double" on both is expected of today's trumpet players.

- Pay attention to and respect the conductor.

Fingering Chart

This page presents you with the *fingering positions* on the trumpet from pedal "C" to double high "C." Certainly this does not mean that you have to play all of these notes as a beginner or as part of your daily training. This information serves only as a reference for the *preferred* fingerings. Later, you will learn that there are several alternate positions for many notes, but the fingerings included here are those you have to learn *first* and should always be kept in mind as the *preferred fingerings*.

Never think you possess the absolute truth regarding intonation. Pitch is in the atmosphere enveloping the whole orchestra, and you have to adjust accordingly.

Warm-Up

It is essential to warm up gradually, without abusing the muscles (especially the muscles of the face). Observe how an athlete prepares his muscles before competing or training, and follow his strategies. Would he attempt to break world records as soon as he arrives on the field? I don't think so! The preparation of his muscles is gradual, starting with slow, easy movements. Warming up is nothing more than awakening half-asleep muscles that need to get put back into action. This principle is perfectly applicable to our profession. Although I don't believe that there is only one way to warm up, there is at least a basic principle that should not be broken: *Avoid brusque or excessive volume at the beginning of the warm-up.* Ignoring this principle could cause a perennial injury of the muscles around the lips.

My routine usually begins by buzzing into the mouthpiece softly. Afterwards, with the instrument, I almost always play "second line G".

Then I proceed up and down the staff, little by little, always staying soft.

I continue my warm-up by playing some flexibility exercises. (Now the tongue is getting involved.) Then come crescendos and decrescendos. This way, the air column starts its function and the complete system will be ready for "startup." It is then that I feel prepared, either to practice or to play without risking any muscle damage or strain. A good warm-up is shown below.

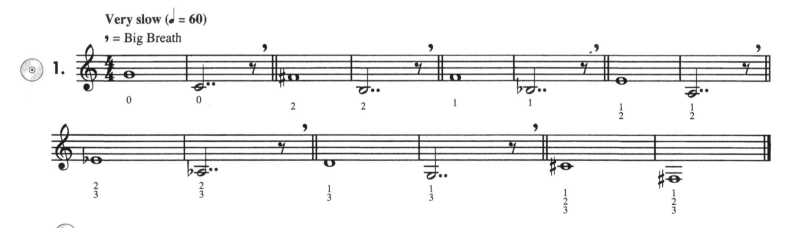

This symbol indicates recorded example.

Pedal notes and scales are good exercises for a "cool-down," which is needed after practice or a performance. It gives the muscles a chance to come back to a relaxed and normal state.

Long Tones/Pedal Tones

These studies are appropriate to include at this early stage, to familiarize you with pedal tones. If you learn how to play them from the very start, your embouchure will take better form, and as a result your sound will be full, clean, big, and clear from the very beginning. The whole-note studies at the beginning of this first book may seem tedious and also difficult because they demand a lot of concentration, effort, and a great desire to accomplish them. They are, however, *very* important. They are the very skills that will "set" the sound and actually create the embouchure that you will need for the rest of your musical life.

Do not believe those who consider pedal tones (like the pedal "E" in bars 5–6 below and pedal "C" in bars 7–8) to be impossible. Pedal tones help establish a correctly positioned embouchure. The result is a strong foundation that allows complicated passages to be played in the future. These notes *are* difficult to play at first, but don't worry. *Try* to play them from the very start; you will become familiar with these notes and they *will* become a lot easier as time goes by.

In order to play pedal notes, and actually to play the instrument in general, it is necessary to keep the throat in an open position by using the syllable "ah." The release of the air is regulated by the tongue, which should be in a flat position, at the bottom of the mouth. You must think as though you were going to sing the notes, pronouncing the open syllable "ah" all the time. *Think* as though you were going to *sing the note.*

Try to practice all these exercises, and also the warm-up first, with the mouthpiece only, then with the instrument. Remember that *the function of the trumpet is to amplify the sound that you make with the mouthpiece.*

It is important to establish this principle. As you play through this entire exercise, you will notice that your embouchure will become stronger, your perception of intonation will be more defined, and your tone quality will increase day by day.

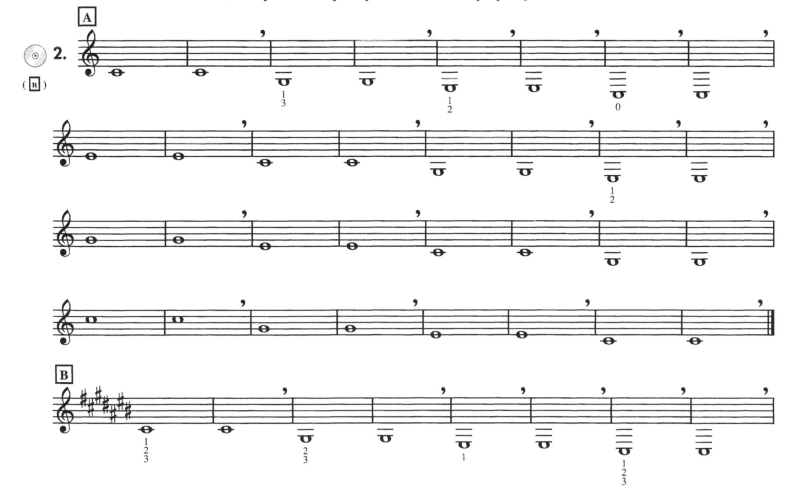

K

L

M

Attack

These are the first studies on the subject of the *attack*. This section concentrates on learning how to make a clear and clean attack by pronouncing the syllable "tu."

Later you will learn several other types of articulations and attacks, but this attack, using syllable "tu," is the *main* one used. Perfecting it will result in an ability to always produce a fundamental clean and clear attack.

Crescendo and Diminuendo

Playing notes with *crescendos* and *diminuendos* teaches you how to control the air column. Additionally, it helps you improve the quality of the sound and requires maintenance of exact intonation at any dynamic level.

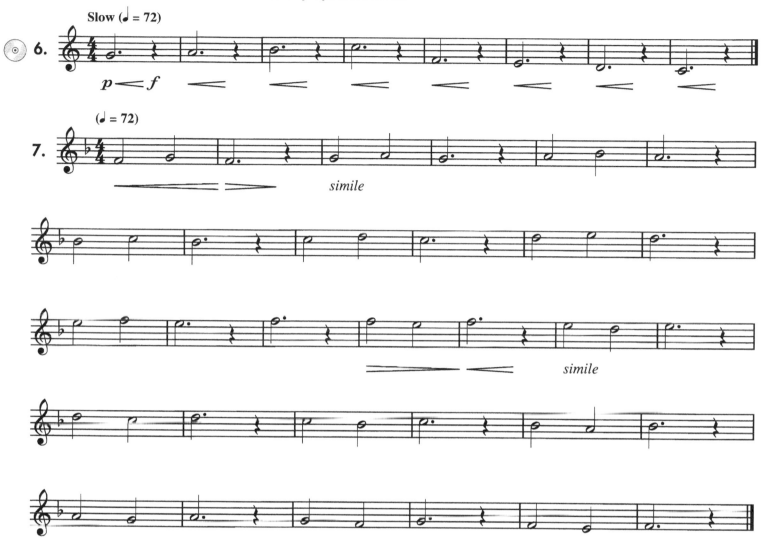

Daily Dynamics

Practice this exercise every day. Playing *dynamics* is essential to learn control of the wind and is fundamental in the development of tone quality.

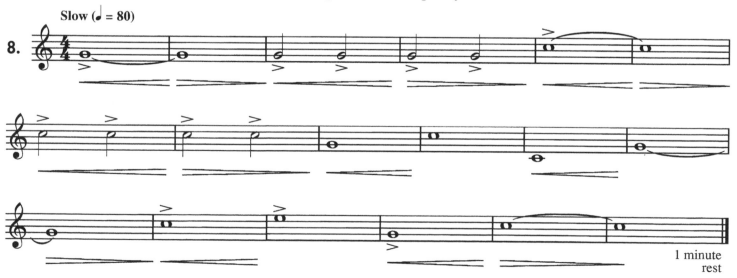

1 minute rest

1 minute
rest

Articulation

Articulation studies with *rhythmic* variations.

(6 clicks)

Arban Staccato Studies

Mastery of this group of lessons from the Arban book is of extreme importance if you wish to develop the use of *staccato*. Numbers 15 and 16 add the challenge of changing key signatures, and number 17 incorporates staccato eighth notes.

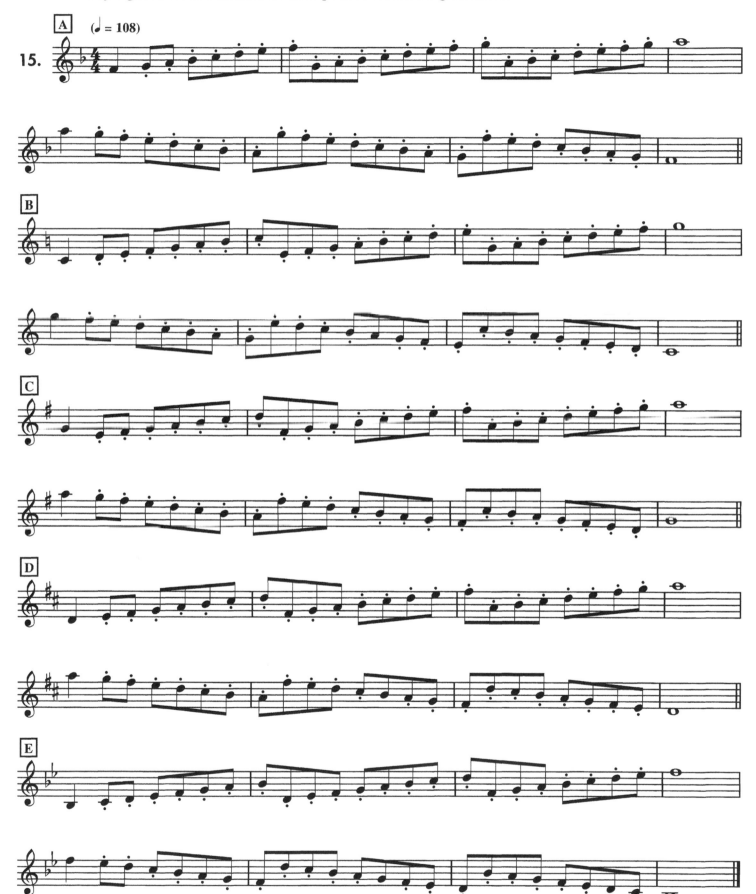

K

L

M

17. (♩ = 96)

simile

Summary Thus Far

This section serves as a *summary* of all you have learned so far. All the major keys are included, as well as different *rhythmic figures*.

19. ($\frac{1}{2}$ = 82)

Rhythmic Figures

This section focuses on learning two rhythmic figures often found in quarter-note meters:

eighth note-quarter note *syncopation*:

and *dotted-eighth-and-sixteenth* figures:

Subdivide the beats into the smallest note value used in the rhythmic figure:

Be careful to avoid subdivision into three:

when the figure is actually to be divided into four:

simile

Tempo di Marcia (= 116)

22.

simile

Allegro moderato (= 108)

23.

simile

26.

27.

Staccato

Staccato studies in all keys.

Staccato Scales

Ascending and *descending scales* in staccato. Use the metronome!

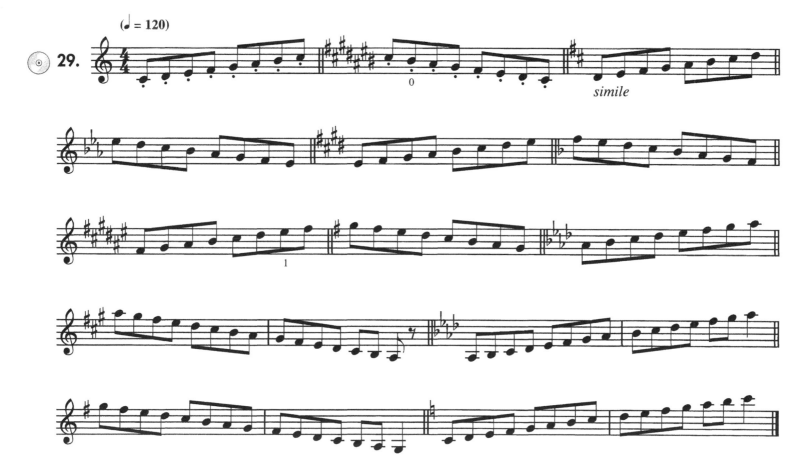

($\quad$ = 120)

29.

0

simile

1

Staccato Octaves

Staccato exercises in *octaves*. Pay particular attention to intonation.

Staccato in 6/8 with Accidentals

This is the first study in a 6/8 time signature. Play it staccato. This piece also provides an excellent challenge in reading *accidentals*.

simile

Flexibility

This section, which begins with some Arban exercises and continues with studies I have written, is included for the purpose of developing *flexibility*. Practice the exercises with a metronome, and pay particular attention to the movement of the tongue, which is crucial for flexibility.

The fundamental role of the tongue is to move the pitch of the tones upward or downward simply by pronouncing the syllables "A-E-I":

A   (Ah)   =   f*a*ther
E   (Eh)   =   r*e*d
I   (Ee)   =   p*i*zza

("A" for low-register notes, "E" for medium, "I" for high.) By pretending you are *singing* these vowels mentally, you will move the tongue to the correct position for the desired pitch.

If the lips alone were involved in changing pitch, you would achieve only lip fatigue, and the resulting intervals would have a poor sound and be out of tune.

The tongue is in charge of pitch, and therefore of intonation.

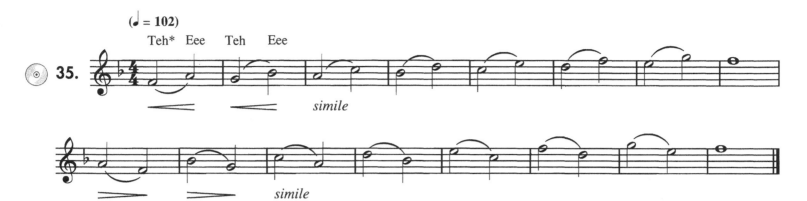

35.

Teh* Eee Teh Eee

($\quad$ = 102)

simile

simile

* Exercises 35-38 should be practiced using the syllables *Teh Eee* with a little more air on the top note.

36.

($\quad$ = 102)

simile

simile

37.

($\quad$ = 102)

simile

simile

38.

($\quad$ = 102)

simile

simile

Legato and Staccato

Practice exercise 41 alternating *legato* and *staccato*, as indicated.

* Continue this pattern, working down chromatically through all valve combinations.

Chromatic Scales

Practice these *chromatic scales* with a metronome, and not any faster than you're able; as you master them at one speed, increase the tempo and play them again. Be sure that every pitch is clean, that the time values of all notes are the same, and that the transfer from one note to another is absolutely clear.

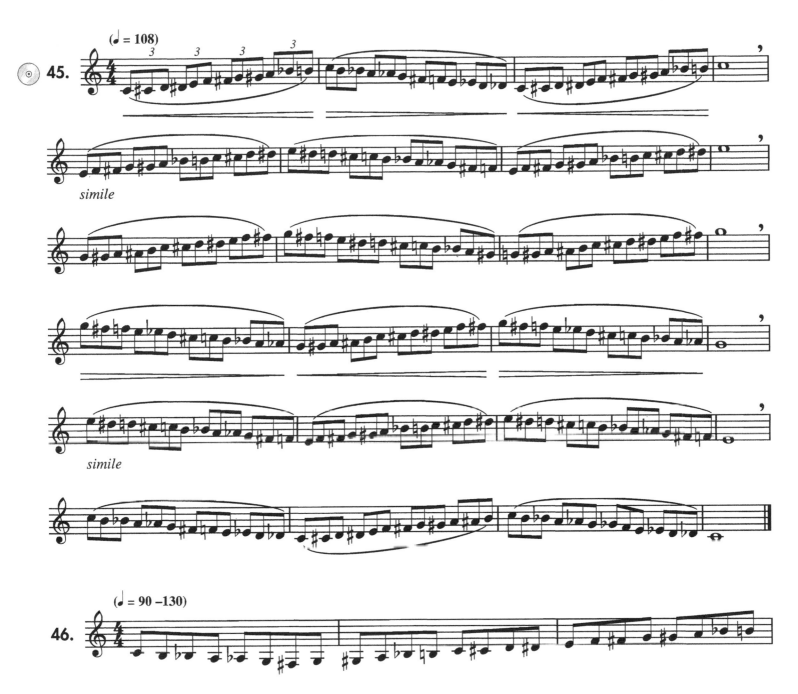

48.

simile

simile

49. ($\quad$ = 112)

simile

simile

Duets

It is important that from the beginning you learn how to play listening to the other part, coordinating rhythm and intonation. Play these duets as if they were small musical pieces, paying special attention to the dynamics and phrasing.

SACRED SONG

Portniansky

AIR BY GRÉTRY

44

AIR BY BEETHOVEN

Andante con moto

52.

MARCH

De Gouy

53.

GERMAN SONG

Kücken

CARNIVAL OF VENICE

Allegro moderato (♩. = 72)

55.

CAVATINA FROM "SOMNAMBULA"

Bellini

Andante moderato

56.

AIR FROM "SOMNAMBULA"

Bellini

57.

WALTZ FROM "PURITANI"

Bellini

58.

3 Stylistic Pieces

The following studies present new rhythmic and musical challenges. Concentrate and pay close attention to the different keys and articulations.

61.

Détaché

This exercise has been written in order to teach what is known as *détaché*, which is simply French for "detached":

It is an articulation midway between legato and staccato, in which the note is clearly separated from the one that follows, but is not shortened as much as a staccato note.

This is a special articulation commonly used in the baroque style. It should be practiced as much as staccato and other articulations.

Piccolo Trumpet in A

Review

Here is a short piece to review what you have learned throughout this book.

Conclusion

In order to conclude this first book, I would like to remind you that your improvement will depend on how much discipline you apply during practice.

Practice is a *daily* task and must be done with concentration, dedication, determination, and a good, positive attitude! You must practice with a mind fixed on the idea that you're doing everything possible to become a musician, an artist who has the technical ability to easily express the ideas that you have in your head.

There really cannot be enough technique. Don't let yourself be confused by those who say that technique spoils a good performance or that it's not necessary to have a lot of technique to be a good performer. I am completely in disagreement with these opinions. The development of technique will never be enough; exactly the opposite is true.

Regarding taste? You will find that taste takes form along the way. It will grow in conjunction with the organization of your ideas, with the emphasis you place on tone color, rhythmic variations, general dynamics, and expression. This ultimate element is essential to the extent that it helps grasp the audience so they can understand and feel the message you are trying to send.

For this reason, a solid technique and a beautiful tone enable the audience to appreciate and enjoy the musical message. These are the necessary means by which we communicate with the audience.

I wish you the best in your musical endeavors, and a brilliant future to all of you who love the trumpet and care for music. Practice with love, devotion, and enthusiasm.

GOOD LUCK!

Acknowledgements

I want to thank Hal Leonard Corporation for giving me the opportunity to put together this project and for providing such professionalism and expertise. A very special thanks to my good friend and great trumpter professor Bob Karon for his dedication and relentless support in the completion of these books. I must mention Alfredo Perez and thank him for his help in the recording of this project. I would also like to acknowledge and thank the people at Schilke Music for all of their support and encouragement.

Please support: Arturo Sandoval's "Dizzy Gillespie Trumpet Scholar Award" at the Lionel Hampton School of Music, University of Idaho. Phone: (208) 885-6765

Arturo Sandoval is managed by: Turi's Music Enterprises Inc. c/o Carl C. Valldejuli 101 South Royal Poinciana Miami Springs, FL 33166 phone (305) 885-5200 fax (305) 884-6766.

Arturo Sandoval records on GRP Records, and performs on a Schilke X3 Trumpet with a Bach 3C mouth piece.

Arturo Sandoval

The arrival of celebrated trumpet player Arturo Sandoval has been joyfully applauded throughout the jazz and classical music communities. Granted political asylum in July 1990, Sandoval, his wife and teenage son made their new home in Miami, Florida. A protégé of the legendary jazz master Dizzy Gillespie, Sandoval was born in Artemisa, a small town on the outskirts of Havana, Cuba, on November 6, 1949, just two years after Gillespie became the first musician to bring Latin influences into American Jazz. Sandoval began studying classical trumpet at the age of twelve, but it didn't take him long to catch the excitement of the jazz world. He has since evolved into one of the world's most acknowledged guardians of jazz trumpet and flugelhorn, as well as a renowned classical artist.

Sandoval was a founding member of the Grammy-winning group Irakere, whose explosive mixture of jazz, classical, rock and traditional Cuban music caused a sensation throughout the entertainment world. In 1981, he left Irakere to form his own band, which garnered enthusiastic praise from critics and audiences all over Europe and Latin America. Sandoval was voted Cuba's Best Instrumentalist from 1982 to 1990.

Before founding Irakere, Sandoval performed with the Cuban Orchestra of Modern Music. He was presented as a guest artist with the BBC Symphony in London and the Leningrad Symphony in Russia. Since his defection, Sandoval has increased his classical performances world-wide including performances with the National Symphony, L.A. Philharmonic, Toledo Symphony, Oklahoma Symphony, and Atlanta Symphony. His classical artistry has earned him the respect and friendship of Maurice André and Adolph Herseth, two of the world's foremost trumpeters.

As a professor, Sandoval performed at the Conservatoire de Paris, the Tchaikovsky Conservatory in the Soviet Union, U.C. Santa Barbara, University of Miami, University of Wisconsin, Purdue University, and at many other institutions in the United States, Europe, and Latin America. Currently, he serves with a full professorship at Florida International University, and maintains one of the most extensive educational programs in the industry with approximately fifty performances and clinics per year. There are two scholarships associated with Sandoval, the "Arturo Sandoval's Dizzy Gillespie Trumpet Scholar Award" at the University of Idaho, and the "Sandoval Trumpet Scholarship" at the Central Oklahoma University.

Sandoval was a featured artist in the acclaimed Dizzy Gillespie United Nation Orchestra, as well as the orchestra's 1992 Grammy-winning album, *Live at Royal Festival Hall*. He has performed with Billy Cobham, Woody Herman, Woody Shaw, Herbie Hancock, Michel Legrand, Stan Getz, and John Williams at the Boston Pops. His playing also can be heard on Dave Grusin's soundtrack for "Havana", in the "Mambo Kings" soundtrack with his Grammy nominated composition "Mambo Caliente", and in the soundtrack of "The Perez Family". His diverse style and versatility can also be heard on albums by the *GRP All Star Big Band,* and Gloria Estefan's *Into The Light* and *Mi Tierra*.

RECORDINGS BY
ARTURO SANDOVAL

Flight To Freedom
GRP Records
GRD-9634

I Remember Clifford
GRP Records
GRD-9668

Dream Come True
GRP Records
GRD-9701

Danzon (Dance On)
GRP Records
GRD-9761

The Classical Album
RCA Victor
09026-62661-2